A PERSONALIST COSMOLOGY

ORIENTATION TO THE CORE THEOLOGY OF THE URANTIA BOOK

David Kantor

Urantia Book Films Press
Lakewood, Colorado
2026

Urantia Book Films Press

ISBN 979-8-218-93545-0
Published In association with
Rocky Mountain Spiritual Fellowship
Boulder, Colorado

Disclaimer
This book makes reference to concepts from The Urantia Book.
The interpretations, commentary, and views expressed herein
are solely those of the author and do not necessarily represent
the views of The Urantia Book Fellowship or any other reader
organization or publisher.

First Edition 2026
Cover Art: David Kantor, Midjourney
Urantia Book Films Press
Lakewood, Colorado, USA
admin@UrantiaBookFilms.org

This monograph was constructed
utilizing collaborative AI

A sower went forth to sow . . .

TABLE OF CONTENTS

PREFACE

There is but one God: In him we live, move, and have our being.

If this is true, then reality is neither a heap of unrelated facts nor a battle-field of rival meanings. There is only one world—deeply mysterious, often difficult, sometimes tragic, yet ultimately coherent and rational.

Though our knowledge is limited, the cosmos cannot be without form. The mind's confidence that things can be understood reflects a correspondence between thought and an underlying order that precedes us, sustains us, and makes understanding possible at all.

The Urantia Book does not present itself as another compartment of belief competing for attention within the modern marketplace of ideas. It offers *a model of reality—an interpretive architecture* within which domains too often held apart may be brought into relation: cosmic order and human experience; moral striving and intellectual honesty; science and religion; freedom and destiny. Its claim is not to replace these domains, but to situate them within a single, intelligible horizon.

Any initial evaluation of The Urantia Book should therefore rest on the integrity of the model it advances: its internal coherence, its explanatory reach, and its capacity to render the world intelligible without flattening its depth or diminishing its mystery.

The Urantia Book resists one-pass comprehension and doctrinal closure. Its worldview comes most fully into focus not through summary or assent, but through lived alignment with the values it discloses—within a personalist, relational framework that must be inhabited over time.

Who This Book is For

This book is written for readers who are comfortable with theological reflection, historical development, and the limits of literalism, who are interested in becoming more familiar with The Urantia Book and its cosmology.

It also will provide a range of new insights for experienced readers of The Urantia Book who have lived with it long enough to sense that its deepest gift is not a set of isolated teachings, but a coherent world—an inhabitable architecture of reality that can be entered, tested, and slowly internalized.

This book also is intended to provide a credible entry point for conversation: a way to bring Urantia Book concepts into responsible dialog with theologically or philosophically informed skeptics or seekers without turning the book into either a private dialect or a public embarrassment.

The aim is explication without dilution—terms, distinctions, and frames that speak across traditions while preserving The Urantia Book's personalist cosmology in its full depth.

If you are interested in anything having to do with the confluence between The Urantia Book and contemporary theological dialog, this book is for you.

After reading this present volume, you will be better equipped to:

» Explore The Urantia Book as a model of reality apart from belief or rejection of its claims
» Value structure as a precursor to understanding detail
» Grasp the essence of The Urantia Book using common philosophical and theological language
» Avoid becoming lost in The Urantia Book's encyclopedic surface

This volume will not:

» Summarize The Urantia Book
» Argue for its authority or truth
» Ask you to replace existing beliefs, faith, or theological commitments
» Rely on circular argument or Urantia-internal self-validation
» Require prior assent to The Urantia Book's claim to be revelation

The Road Ahead

This volume focuses on three conceptual strands that provide the core of Urantia Book ontology. The interdependence of *personalism, ascendant experience,* and *universe administration* constitute the backbone of the text, providing context for the full scope of The Urantia Book's sweeping cosmology.

Here is a brief overview of The Urantia Book's personalist cosmology:

Chapter 1—The Fragmented State of the 21st-Century Western Mind: Diagnoses late-modern disorientation as the loss of an inhabitable framework for thought, showing how information, process, and spiritual seeking become exhausting when they lack a stable horizon of meaning

Chapter 2—Inhabitation: Introduces The Urantia Book as an architectural unveiling meant to be entered and lived within

Chapter 3—Architecture of the Inhabitable Framework: Defines the 3-strand backbone ontology and articulates the book's personalist profile

Chapter 4—Strand 1, Personalism: Develops personalism as an ontological commitment, centering divine indwelling as the interior coordination that makes participation, value-discovery, soul-formation, and co-created destiny intelligible

Chapter 5—Strand 2, Ascension: Presents ascension as the progressive enhancement of personality experience, noting that values embraced in choice-making are conserved and integrated into destiny

Chapter 6—Strand 3, Universe Administration: Explains administration as the mediating architecture that assures a universe environment capable of fostering growth

Chapter 7—The Fractal-like Architecture of Universe Administration: Develops the three-strand ontology as a conceptual nucleus operating across scalable universe realities, supporting relationship, growth, and coordination across widely differing levels

Chapter 8—Calibration in a Personal Universe: Defines calibration as personality orientation provided by spiritually stable value-references integrating divine indweller, the person of Jesus, universe administration, and the Father as scale-differentiated calibration presences that keep meaning cosmically coherent

Chapter 9—Jesus of Nazareth as Embodied Demonstration: Presents Jesus as the embodied demonstration and lived calibration point in whom the three strands become visible and practicable within conditions of human existence

Chapter 10—The World Transforming Implications: Traces how a personalist, indwelling-mediated, ascendant framework reinterprets politics, technology, education, economics, spirituality, and history as domains of relational stewardship and value-bearing responsibility

Appendix I—Schools of Personalism Compared: Provides a concise taxonomy of major personalist schools, positioning "relational-ontological personalism" as an apt descriptor for The Urantia Book's personalism

Appendix II—Orthodox-Trinitarian Personalism: Places The Urantia Book's relational-ontological personalism in disciplined dialogue with Orthodox-Trinitarian personalism, clarifying shared relational grammar as well as points where cosmological logics and ontologies diverge

Appendix III—The Roots of the Personalist Heritage: Identifies representative figures and trajectories that establish the ontological grammar of both Orthodox-Trinitarian personalism and Catholic personalism, comparing them with The Urantia Book's relational-ontological personalism

Appendix IV—Some Theological Vocabulary for Readers of The Urantia Book: Defines key terms used in this present volume to stabilize categories and prevent interpretive drift

Chapter 1:
The Fragmented State
of the 21st-Century Western Mind

Contemporary life is curiously starved of *orientation*. What is increasingly absent is not intelligence, sincerity, or effort, but a frame of reference capable of being internalized rather than merely thought about.

The absence of inhabitable frameworks explains much of the modern condition: why information overwhelms rather than clarifies, why attempts at growth exhaust rather than fulfill, and why spiritual seeking so often produces intensity without continuity.

Without a structure capable of providing continuity for the interpretation of experience over time, life fragments into episodes, reactions, and improvisations. Meaning must be improvised continuously instead of discovered progressively.

Information Without Meaning Is Disorienting

Information acquires meaning only within an interpretive framework of values. Absent such a framework, information may be abundant and precise, yet fails to orient life. Facts accumulate without synthesis, reactions replace understanding, and knowledge grows while wisdom recedes.

The modern individual is therefore not uninformed but misaligned—data-literate and articulate, yet lacking a stable horizon of meaning.

Process Without Purpose, Becoming Without Direction

Contemporary culture speaks enthusiastically about process, celebrating change, evolution, and self-development. Yet this embrace of becoming is paired with resistance to teleology—any shared account of purpose, direction, or fulfillment.

The result is drift. Growth is encouraged without orientation; experience accumulates without integration into a coherent narrative. Individuals are urged to keep evolving. But without an inhabitable framework for evaluating experience, growth becomes endless adaptation to changing conditions. Process alone is not progressively livable without orientation to direction and purpose.

Spiritual Life Without an Inhabitable Framework

The absence of inhabitable frameworks is most acute in personal spiritual life, where intellectual disorientation affects identity, purpose, commitment, and endurance. Contemporary spirituality is often eclectic and experiential—open and sincere, yet detached from long-term commitment. Spiritual practices are sampled rather than inhabited; spirituality becomes a sequence of encounters instead of a place of dwelling.

Lacking a model that integrates experience over time, spiritual insights remain isolated.

Living Without a World to Live In

The psychological costs are substantial. Anxiety becomes chronic, decision fatigue accumulates, and moral development gives way to moral uncertainty. The self must decide what matters and then live out its choices without any larger framework of reinforcement to fall back on.

Meaning survives only as long as it's useful for navigating daily life. This is analogous to choosing to be honest while believing that there is no real right or wrong, no larger order, and no reason honesty should matter beyond my personal preference.

What should feel like living inside a stable world becomes constant self-management. No finite person can endure this indefinitely. Without an inhabitable framework that precedes and enables the rational ordering of personal values, life collapses into perpetual improvisation and becomes a task rather than a home.

Chapter 2:
Inhabitation

We in late-modern Western culture inhabit a world defined by constant change, fractured meaning, and the erosion of shared narratives. Stability has yielded to velocity, coherence to immediacy, and lack of orientation has become the default condition rather than the exception.

The shift required is not primarily informational but architectural. It concerns how one faces reality. Much of modern consciousness treats reality as an impersonal milieu that one is forced to deal with—an external field against which the self must construct meaning. Individuals come to see themselves as isolated units, the world as a hostile environment, and significance as a private project. Life is navigated tactically; meaning is assembled situation by situation; spirituality becomes episodic rather than enduring.

To thrive in a turbulent environment, an inhabitable frame of reference is not a luxury but a necessity. Without a structure capable of stabilizing identity, values, and purpose amid change, individuals absorb cultural volatility emotionally, at the cost of anxiety and exhaustion. The needed shift in perspective is architectural: from isolation to belonging, from improvisation to participation, and from episodic spirituality to life within an inhabitable, personal cosmos.

From Secularism to Existentialism to Personalism

When transcendent reference points are removed—when God, teleology, and objective metaphysical order are no longer credible—the remaining task of thought is to account for human existence as it is actually experienced. Existentialism describes the condition that results. In this sense, existentialism is less a choice than a consequence: It is the inevitable philosophical endpoint of secularism unrestrained by spiritual insight.

As transcendence is eclipsed, objective reality shrinks to the immediate situation of the individual. With no cosmic background, meanings become situationally derived. Values no longer disclose themselves as objective or binding but are constructed relative to situational needs. Purpose, deprived of any given horizon, is no longer discovered but fabricated by the self.

Existentialism is what philosophy looks like when secularism has finished its work. It's the moment of bleakness when modern consciousness becomes fully aware of what life feels like without transcendence, thereby revealing the limits of secular reason itself. Existentialism is the philosophical equivalent of being lost in a vast desert with nothing but the sky for orientation.

This is precisely where personalist and relational ontologies begin—not as denials of existentialism, but as responses to what existentialism reveals and cannot repair on its own. Existentialism acknowledges the radical isolation of the individual. Personalism emerges out of this seeming dead-end: *It focuses on the potential of relationships between those isolated persons as the basis for constructing a coherent account of reality.*

For readers of The Urantia Book, this claim will feel less like a novel theory and more like a clarification of an already-familiar universe—one in which personality is bestowed by God, its identity sustained unchanged over time, and its purpose fulfilled through relationship.

An Inhabitable Framework

An inhabitable framework is a model of reality that a person can recognize as real and actually live within—not merely analyze or assent to at arm's length. It integrates understanding and participation so that meaning emerges through lived alignment rather than inference alone. One comes to know such a framework by inhabiting it.

Inhabitation is inseparable from commitment. This commitment is not a preference for comforting ideas, but an inward, responsible "yes" tested in time—chosen repeatedly under uncertainty, cost, and consequence. Such seriousness is not irrational; it is the form of responsibility appropriate to realities that cannot be possessed as objects, only trusted and enacted.

An inhabitable framework therefore resists two reductions at once. It does not attempt to order life solely through propositions or rules, as though meaning were secured by correct statements. Nor does it dissolve meaning into subjective improvisation, as though reality were only what the self can sustain. Instead, it furnishes a durable environment in which trust, responsibility, choice, and hope remain intelligible across time and experience.

In this sense, an inhabitable framework is less a theory than an environment. The difference may be illustrated simply. A city map may be accurate and informative, but it cannot be lived in. It does not tell you where to wake up, how to move through the day, or how today connects meaningfully to tomorrow. A city itself by contrast, can be *inhabited*. It has rhythms, pathways, and institutions that stabilize life. Meaning arises from living within it over time.

Inhabitation is Not Religious Identity

To inhabit a framework is not to adopt its symbols or speak its language, but *to live from within its organizing imagery.* Inhabitation reshapes how reality is perceived, what is noticed, what is valued, and how choices are made—even when no outward markers are present.

One can take on the social identity of a believer, a scholar, or a worker without actually inhabiting the worldview to which those labels relate. Inhabitation occurs only when a framework becomes the medium through which experience itself is interpreted and processed into new existential meanings and spiritual values.

This distinction matters because The Urantia Book does not seek to confer a new religious identity but to invite inhabitation. Its aim is not to produce readers who think of themselves as Urantia Book believers, but persons whose inner orientation—toward values, relationship, growth, and participation—has been quietly reorganized. Identity can be worn; inhabitation must be lived. The former is visible and reversible; the latter is interior, cumulative, and consequential.

The identity which The Urantia Book fosters is the recognition of oneself as a child of God.

A Profile of The Urantia Book's Inhabitable Framework

It's Personal

Persons are ultimate in value. Personality is the center of identity and free will, discrete as chooser but relational in existence, grounded in an indwelling divine presence that personalizes destiny without overriding freedom of choice.

Personality is ultimate, but not solitary. Personal reality is dually inhabited: Finite personality and divine presence share a single arena of decision and meaning.

It's Relational

Interpersonal relationship is ontologically real rather than merely social or instrumental. Personality cannot express itself in isolation, only through relationships with other persons—mortal and divine.

Relationship is the arena in which personality is expressed, tested, and matured; where values become concrete through mutual recognition, service, forgiveness, and cooperation. Personal growth is therefore inseparable from relational life. Identity deepens through encounter in relationship. Freedom is educated through responsibility to others. Meaning emerges through shared experience.

It's Indwelt

Human personality is made for enduring companionship with a fragment of Deity. It is not absorbed by the Divine Indweller, but neither does it exist meaningfully without it. Real growth is not merely developmental or moral: *It is relational and co-creative.*

Mature personal life unfolds within a shared interior field, where finite will and divine presence cooperate in the work of becoming. Indwelling is not merely one ontological feature among others, added to an already complete human inventory. It is the inward, vertical axis that links temporal personhood to transcendence—the sustaining line along which meanings clarify, values take hold, and destiny becomes more than aspiration. Through it the other elements of the profile become dynamically operative: Relationship deepens beyond sociability; growth acquires direction and experience begins to cohere as an identifiable life rather than a sequence of moments.

The constitutive form of human existence is characterized by the integration of personality and indwelling.

It's Teleological

Existence is oriented toward ends. But destiny is not a prefabricated script waiting to be uncovered. In the Urantia Book model it begins as possibility—resident in the living tension between personality and the Divine Indweller—and it becomes actual only as that possibility is chosen, embodied, and sustained.

The pursuit of God's will, then, is not chiefly submission to an external authority; it is alignment with reality at its deepest generative level: the free consent of the self to what is true, good, and enduring. Destiny is not discovered but *created*—emerging through co-creative action over time as decisions become character, and character becomes a cosmically creative force.

This pursuit is inseparable from indwelling: Indwelling provides the interior presence of guidance, while personality orientation to God's will supplies the direction of growth. Together they define an ontology of indwelt personality participating in purposeful universe unfolding. Growth is not random, and history is not drifting; personality is invited to cooperate intelligently with realizable ends.

It's Developmental

Becoming is normal. Growth is the expected mode of existence, progressing from biological life to moral agency and spiritual destiny, enabled by interior spiritual guidance that works through time, experience, and decision. Growth is not self-generating. Becoming is the progressive synchronization of human choosing and divine leading. The challenge of personal life is to cultivate conditions within which growth can take place.

It's Moral

Values are discovered rather than invented. Moral insight emerges through the alignment of personal choice with a divinely illuminated higher will, not imposed externally but discovered inwardly through lived decision. With regard to values, the mortal mind must discover, recognize, interpret, and choose. Moral insight arises from the tension and dialogue between human intent and indwelt guidance.

It's Participatory

Truth is realized by personality through lived engagement. Participation involves cooperation with an indwelling divine initiative, clarified relationally, and confirmed through experience rather than belief alone. Participation is not only engagement with the world or cosmos, but also with the Divine Indweller.

It's Structured

Reality is ordered and intelligible without being rigid or mechanistic. Personal freedom operates within a meaningful cosmic order, administered but not micromanaged, coordinated without coercion.

It's Integrative

Inner life and outer action form a single field of significance. Thought, values, and behavior are unified around an interior spiritual center of gravity, where divine initiative and human response co-create meaning.

It's Hopeful

The future is real and open. Hope is grounded in the consciousness of indwelling rather than abstract promise; assured by interior continuity rather than external guarantees. *The future is already present in the soul as divine presence.*

The Urantia Book is not providing a metaphysical system, doctrine, or ideology to adopt. It is identifying an already existing inhabitable framework within which discovery and revelation can flourish beyond the boundaries normally defined by science, philosophy and religion. It serves as a platform for the disclosure of cosmic depth and stability which catalyzes personal growth—from evolutionary origins to cosmic citizenship.

Such alignment is the supreme act of orientation: learning to live in consonance with the deep organic flow of reality rather than grasping at metaphysical straws in the surface turbulence. It does not erase individuality; it deepens it. One becomes more fully oneself by choosing within a meaningful teleological horizon, where freedom is not severed from purpose but gathered into it.

We do not create the current. We awaken to its direction, feel its pressure in conscience and in consequence, and begin—haltingly—to set ourselves with it. Like sailors on a vast, living sea, we trim our sails to a movement we cannot fully name: a cosmic flow we only dimly sense, yet can increasingly learn to trust as we move with it.

In Him We Live, Move and Have Our Being

The statement, "In Him we live, move and have our being," is often received as poetic metaphor. Understood ecologically, it is not metaphorical at all. Life does not merely occur within a universe; it is sustained by that universe, moment by moment, through continuous participation in its larger, living order.

Within this framework, there is no clean demarcation between inner life and cosmic reality, because consciousness itself is embedded in a larger field of meaning. The appropriate analogy is ecological rather than mechanical. As in a living ecosystem, boundaries exist, but they are porous and functional, not absolute. Identity is preserved without isolation; participation occurs without absorption. One lives *within* reality in the same way a cell lives within an organism—not as a detachable unit, but as a meaningful participant in a greater, sustaining whole.

CHAPTER 3:
THE ARCHITECTURE OF THE INHABITABLE FRAMEWORK

There are three structural strands that hold The Urantia Book's personalist cosmology intact across its approximately 2,000 pages. *These three strands in their interwoven unity constitute the ontological core of The Urantia Book.*

Personalism — What Is Ultimately Real

Personalism, affirms personality as ontologically primary. Ultimate reality is not understood as impersonal forces, energies, mechanisms, or abstract processes—but by *persons in relationship.* Personality, relationship, and indwelling name the basic terms of what is real. This strand prevents reduction of the cosmos to metaphysics without personhood, to process without subject, or to psychology without ontological depth.

Ascension — Teleological Personal Life in Time and Space

Ascension names the developmental trajectory made possible by a personal universe. It describes how personality moves, grows, and fulfills destiny through experience across time. Ascension is not an added promise appended to personal existence. It is the necessary continuity of a universe that takes personality seriously and conserves the values generated through lived experience.

Universe Administration — Architecture in Service of Personality

Universe administration provides the mediating structure that allows transcendent Deity to be present and effective within finite experience without overwhelming it. Infinity must be scaled, paced, and ordered if finite persons are to encounter it meaningfully. Administration does not replace personal meaning or diminish freedom. *It preserves the conditions under which growth, choice, and development can occur.*

The first two strands—Personalism and Ascension—establish core ontological commitments: what is real, how Deity relates to reality, and what kind of developmental movement personal existence entails. The third strand—Universe Administration—sustains these commitments across time and scale. It provides the ordered environment within which personal reality and ascendant growth can unfold coherently.

Each strand names a necessity required by the other two. Personality without a developmental trajectory would lack fulfillment. Development without conserved values would lack meaning. Both would collapse without an ordered framework capable of mediating transcendence and coordinating growth. No one of the three strands remains intelligible in isolation; their coherence depends on their integrated operation. The next three chapters examine each strand in turn.

CHAPTER 4:
STRAND 1—PERSONALISM

Personalism begins with a simple but radical claim: Reality is not finally explained by things, forces, energies, particles, or systems, but by persons and their relationships. In this view, individuality is not a prison of isolation but a point of entry into relationship; selfhood matures, not by withdrawal from the world, but by participation in it. History becomes more than a sequence of events, ethics more than a set of rules, and faith more than assent to propositions—each becomes a lived drama of persons discovering values together.

Personalism thus offers a way beyond abstraction and alienation, beyond secularism and existentialism—re-centering philosophy, theology, and culture on the dignity, destiny, and relational depth of lived personal life itself.

As previously suggested, personalism for experienced readers of The Urantia Book will feel less like an imported philosophy and more like an articulated clarification of an already-familiar worldview—particularly where the teachings of Jesus have been influential.

Personality as Ontologically Primary

The Urantia Book locates the universe's meaning in personality and its relationships:

» Personality is ontologically primary, bestowed by the Universal Father and divinely indwelt.

» Relationship is cosmologically decisive, spanning human association, divine relation, and realities beyond the present order.

» Growth is teleological, oriented toward destiny through experiential participation rather than attainment of static perfection.

Personalism here is not a psychological description or an ethical preference. It is an ontological claim. Personality is not emergent, epiphenomenal, or constructed from more basic elements. It is neither reducible to mind, soul, consciousness, nor value. Personality originates in purposes beyond creature comprehension and is therefore irreducible. This places personality prior to mind, meaning, and moral valuation.

In this sense, personality is existentially ultimate rather than metaphysically derived. It does not arise from substance, process, or abstraction. It is given.

Faith as Participation

Faith is not primarily belief in propositions but trustful participation in a personal reality actively present within experience. Knowing unfolds through time. It is moral and relational rather than merely conceptual. Truth is not only apprehended; it is lived into.

Ethics as Ontological Alignment

Because reality is personal and purposive, moral action is not a matter of taste, nor merely a social contract. Love, service, forgiveness, and growth are not optional ornaments of character; they are ways of moving with the grain of what is. They name the forms of action that fit a universe ordered around persons and directed toward meaning. Moral insight, then, is not chiefly the discovery of new rules, but the clarifying light that comes when a willing self chooses into coherence with personal reality.

Revelation as Orientation

Revelation is not primarily doctrinal or authoritarian. Its function is *orientational.* It establishes a universe frame within which thinking, choosing, and living can be coherently re-aligned. The authority of revelation is therefore instrumental rather than terminal: It serves personal understanding and growth rather than replacing them.

Unselfish Service as Praxis

Service is not an optional add-on to a personalist worldview; it is the worldview taking bodily form. If reality is finally disclosed in personal relation, then the truth of such a vision cannot remain merely conceptual—it must be enacted. Service is the concrete way a personalist ontology becomes legible in time: the decision to treat persons as irreducible centers of value, not as functions, obstacles, or instruments. It is where "what we say we believe about persons" meets the daily friction of actual persons—needs, limits, misunderstandings, burdens, delays, and ordinary suffering.

In this sense, service is *praxis:* lived interpretation. It is the disciplined practice by which inner orientation becomes outward fidelity. Not charity as sentiment, not activism as identity performance, not "good deeds" as moral bookkeeping—but the steady conversion of insight into conduct, and of conviction into presence. Service tests our metaphysics in the most unforgiving arena: real time, real people, real costs. It is the place where love becomes skillful, where truth becomes patient, where ideals become habits, and where spiritual claims either translate into relational reality or collapse into rhetoric.

Service also functions as a calibrating instrument. It reveals whether our spirituality is drifting into private comfort, aesthetic contemplation, or a merely internal "growth project." When we serve, we are forced out of the dream of self-sufficiency and into the ecology of mutuality: attention becomes responsibility; compassion becomes commitment; insight becomes tact; intention becomes reliability. Service is the practical grammar of personalism—how a universe of persons is honored, one interaction at a time.

The Personalist Teaching of Jesus

Before personalism appears as philosophy, it appears as life. In the teachings of Jesus—most clearly in the Sermon on the Mount—personalism is not argued but assumed. Jesus does not offer a theory of the person. He teaches persons how to live as persons in a world composed of other persons, each bearing irreducible value.

His teachings also are notable for what they do not emphasize: They do not center on law as an external code, identity as a boundary marker, or righteousness as public conformity. Instead, they turn attention inward: toward motive, intention, mercy, reconciliation, and trust. Anger matters as much as violence; reconciliation precedes worship; love extends beyond reciprocity to include the enemy. The moral field Jesus describes is *relational* rather than *transactional*. One's interior orientation toward others becomes decisive.

Here, the Kingdom of Heaven is neither a political arrangement nor a distant metaphysical abstraction. It is a lived relational order—a way persons inhabit reality together. The Beatitudes describe dispositions that reconfigure perception itself: humility, mercy, purity of heart, peacemaking. These are not virtues added onto life; they are ways of being with others that disclose a different texture of reality.

Jesus' teaching therefore presupposes a personalist ontology. Reality is responsive to personal orientation. Meaning emerges through relationship. Moral growth is real, cumulative, and consequential. Persons are not isolated moral agents navigating an impersonal world, but participants within a living moral ecology where choices reverberate across relationships.

From Teaching to Universe Context

What The Urantia Book contributes is not a modification of Jesus' message, but an expansion of its horizon. The personalism implicit in Jesus' teaching—rooted in intimate human relations—is projected onto a vast universe context. The immediate field in which Jesus teaches is disclosed as one level within a reality composed, at every scale, of personal beings in relationship with each other.

Within this expanded frame, the Kingdom Jesus proclaims is no longer confined to moral life on earth or to interior spiritual experience alone. It is revealed as a universe-spanning process in which personal relationships, freely chosen values, and lived meanings are gathered, conserved, and integrated. What Jesus teaches locally—how to live as a person among persons—is unfolded cosmically.

In this way, Jesus' teaching about the Kingdom becomes intelligible as more than ethical instruction. It discloses how reality itself functions when personality is taken seriously. The same relational logic governing forgiveness, service, and love in human life is shown to operate across reality as a whole.

In this sense, the Sermon on the Mount's personalist ethic already contains a grammar of ascension. Jesus' teaching names a teleological horizon in which persons, through relationship, generate enduring values that can be carried forward into the future.

CHAPTER 5:
STRAND 2—ASCENSION

In The Urantia Book, *ascension* names the progressive realization of personal destiny through experiential growth in relationship with God and other persons. Grounded in a personalist ontology, ascension is the actualization of a bestowed personal identity through moral choice, spiritual insight, relational integration, and cooperation with the Divine Indweller.

Ascension does not describe escape from finitude or absorption into impersonal unity. It is fulfillment rather than negation of personality. Finite experience is transformed into enduring values while personal identity remains intact and increasingly unified with its transcendent source. Ascension is not the evolution of personality, but the progressive enlargement of what personality has become capable of containing and expressing.

One way to picture this movement is as a developmental alternation between meaning and value. As meanings are grasped, higher values become visible. When those values are embodied in thought and action, new meanings emerge. The pattern repeats over time: Meaning illuminates value; value discloses deeper meaning. Growth proceeds through this sequential movement, not by sudden transcendence or static perfection.

The rate of personal development corresponds to the growth of coherence between personal will and divine purpose. Ascension is therefore neither automatic nor imposed. It unfolds through free choice, experience, and sustained alignment.

Significance for the Individual

The Meaning of Ascension

Ascension names the core movement of personal existence: the progressive growth of finite persons toward deeper meaning, spiritualized values, and integrated living. It is not limited to post-mortem destiny or a mythic afterlife narrative. It is an ontological description of how personal reality is structured to be entered, traversed, and increasingly unified.

Ascent begins within time. Moral decision, spiritual responsiveness, and experiential learning are its starting points. Survival is the continuity of growth. Destiny is not static completion but unending participation in an enlarging reality.

Ascension reframes life teleologically:

» Existence is oriented toward an end: Growth has direction and culmination.
» Meaning arises from destination: The arc of becoming supplies coherence to the present.
» Struggle, error, effort, and choice are not obstacles to destiny: They are the means by which destiny is achieved.
» Present limitations are not failures of being: They are conditions of becoming.

Because ascension is experiential, moral choice matters structurally:

» Choices form character.
» Character consolidates values.
» Accrued values are conserved.
» Freedom is neither swallowed by determinism nor isolated in existential autonomy. It operates within a purposive order. Ordinary acts of fidelity, service, patience, and growth in love therefore possess ontological significance. They are not private virtues; they are contributions to personal and cosmic development.

Faith as Forward Trust

Within an ascendant universe, faith functions as confidence in the reliability of reality itself: that growth is meaningful, that values are conserved, and that personal striving participates in something enduring. Faith is dynamic rather than static: trust in a future not yet experienced, grounded in a present reality already encountered.

Significance for the Evolution of Civilization

Civilization as Collective Ascension

Ascension scales upward. Civilizations develop not primarily through technology, power, or efficiency, but through the cumulative moral and spiritual maturation of persons.

Institutions, cultures, and traditions function as provisional scaffolds for character growth. When they support personal development, they flourish; when they obstruct it, they decay. History is therefore neither linear progress nor meaningless repetition. It is uneven, moral, and developmental.

Social Structures Judged by Growth Outcomes

Societies are evaluated not by dominance or longevity, but by how well they foster:

- » Personality development
- » Moral responsibility and truth-seeking
- » Freedom coordinated with coherence

Civilizational advance is measured by integration of character and conscience rather than institutional reach. The Urantia Book does not promise social transformation through information transfer, but through the gradual interior transformation of persons whose lives then re-pattern culture.

Integration Without Homogenization

Because ascension is personal, civilization does not advance by erasing difference. Unity is achieved through integration at higher levels of meaning, not through uniformity. Distinct persons and cultures remain differentiated while coordinated within shared values and purposes. This yields a non-totalitarian vision of planetary development.

Ontological Significance of Ascension

Hope Without Naivety

Ascension grounds hope without illusion. Growth is real, but it is slow, fragile, and purchased through struggle. Nothing is automatic; advance is cooperative. In this light, hope is neither utopian expectation nor cynical retreat, but faithfulness informed by a long horizon.

Ascension is The Urantia Book's account of how personal agency is woven into the structure of reality itself. For the individual, it renders life a meaningful career of becoming. For civilization, it redefines progress as the cumulative maturation of persons and the social forms they evolve.

History thus becomes neither accidental nor predetermined, but participatory—slow, moral, and profoundly personal.

CHAPTER 6:
STRAND 3—UNIVERSE ADMINISTRATION

In The Urantia Book, *universe administration* names the cosmic infrastructure providing supportive background for an integrated, ordered cosmos—one teeming with intelligent life and multiple levels of being. It insures the integrity of free personal choice, value discovery, and relational continuity across ascending levels of development.

Administrative structures in a personal universe do not subordinate personality to mechanism. They *coordinate* universe processes in service of personal ends, ensuring that evolutionary change remains meaningful and that finite achievement can be conserved. In this way, universe administration is the mediating framework through which a personalist ontology becomes operational at cosmic scale: Freedom, order, and purpose coexist without reducing persons to products—or God to process.

If infinity were encountered without mediation, it would either overwhelm finitude or negate the very conditions—distance, duration, and freedom—within which persons can grow. Administration therefore operates as graduated mediation: sustaining contact in forms creatures can receive, so that transcendence is real and effective without becoming crushing or growth-eliminating.

Collapse and the Necessity for Mediation

When transcendence is not carefully mediated, it collapses in one of two opposite directions, both historically observable.

In an upward collapse, revealed transcendence overwhelms mortal finitude. The result is absorption into mysticism, fatalism, fear of God, devaluation of moral struggle, and the rise of religious authority. Experience loses relevance; finite personality ceases to function as a choosing subject. Distinct personal identity may dissolve into an undifferentiated divine or cosmic whole. Growth ends because there is no longer a "someone" to grow.

In this collapse, revelation becomes authoritarian. Personal agency is abandoned, and God is experienced as overpowering rather than relational. Infinity consumes finitude.

In a downward collapse, transcendence dissolves into immanent closure. God is reduced to psychology, ethics, or symbolism. Ultimate meaning is lost, values become situational, and shared spiritual orientation disintegrates. Personal religious experience becomes privatized or episodic, lacking any integrating horizon.

Here, experience loses orientation beyond itself. Values lose objective grounding, and growth becomes circular or merely therapeutic. Transcendence evaporates into finite relativity; revelation becomes metaphor rather than disclosure.

Collapse pressure is unavoidable. Mortal beings grow by making value choices, and values require contrast in order to be visible: truth and error, good and evil, effort and achievement. Contrast is the condition that allows value to become lived significance. Without careful mediation, this necessary tension becomes destructive.

Universe administration exists to preserve what may be called *a zone of managed tension*: the narrow range in which freedom is real, growth is possible, and neither overwhelming transcendence nor reductive immanent closure negate personal experience.

Administration ensures that transcendence is revealed gradually, selectively, and developmentally. This prevents upward collapse. At the same time, transcendence is not delivered as raw exposure to infinity, but in forms that require personal response—meanings, values, purpose, pattern, and destiny—thereby preventing downward collapse.

Managing this tension between abandonment of personal agency and loss of transcendence is an intrinsic function of universe administration. It regulates the relationship between existential Deity and ascending mortals, keeping experience within growth-producing boundaries while providing stimulation through metered revelation.

The Role of Epochal Revelation

Within The Urantia Book's historical account, epochal revelation may appear when collapse pressure exceeds levels compatible with spiritually vital cultural continuity.

When transcendence is mythologized, religion becomes institutionalized. Shared worldviews fragment, and downward collapse accelerates. Conversely, when transcendence is absolutized beyond the conditions of time and daily life, upward collapse becomes inevitable.

Against downward collapse, epochal revelation restores vertical depth. It reintroduces a coherent cosmology, a shared moral horizon, and a narrative of destiny capable of integrating experience.

Against upward collapse, revelation restores habitable scale. Transcendence is re-mediated through personal, historical, and experiential forms that preserve freedom and developmental pacing.

In both cases, epochal revelation functions to prevent the cultural and religious pathologies that arise when transcendence and immanent closure lose their growth-producing tension. It rebuilds narrative scaffolding within which experience can cohere, moral insight can generalize, and spiritual intuition can become sharable without distortion.

Universe administration regulates conditions, not outcomes. Outcomes are the result of free will choices made by persons.

Administration as Developmental Stewardship

Universe administrators may be likened to gardeners. They prepare environments, working within the constraints of climate and season. Gardening presumes patience across time, not immediate results. Conditions are optimized so that inherent potentials may express themselves.

Revelation, meaning, and personal development cannot be externally forced. They must emerge from the center of free will choice. A viable developmental environment therefore includes risk, variation, failure, and recovery. Universe administration tolerates error, sin, and evil as the transient cost of freedom.

In The Urantia Book, universe administration assures the integrity of cosmic architecture. This is not metaphorical but structural. Every level of existence is embedded within a larger system. No being is isolated or self-sufficient. Character growth occurs through relationship, cooperation, and participation. Higher values emerge through integration rather than domination.

One of the most frequently misunderstood aspects of The Urantia Book—its extensive hierarchies—functions ecologically rather than competitively. Each level supports, coordinates, and stabilizes those below it. Authority exists to enable development, not to extract obedience.

Within this ecological framework, personality functions as a keystone reality. Everything else—energy, mind, spirit—serves as environmental support for growth and decision. This is how the universe can be cosmically vast without becoming impersonal.

In a universe that is personal, relational, and developmental, coherence cannot be achieved through centralized control, impersonal law, or static hierarchy. Any structure capable of coordinating such a reality must preserve freedom while sustaining growth across vastly different scales.

For this reason, the administrative order disclosed in The Urantia Book operates through relational patterns that repeat across scale without distortion.

CHAPTER 7:
THE FRACTAL-LIKE ARCHITECTURE
OF UNIVERSE ADMINISTRATION

In this model, authority is a recursive service. It always exists for growth. Power flows downward as support, not upward as extraction. Leadership recapitulates the same role at every level. Thus, across levels of interpersonal reality:

» Ultimate reality sustains all that exists.
» Administrating centers sustain the integrity and developmental conditions of their domains.
» Civil leadership sustains the social order within which persons can mature, cooperate, and flourish.
» Households and institutions sustain local worlds through care, formation, and shared responsibility.
» Persons sustain one another through love, fidelity, and practical service.

This fractal-like architecture of life extends into biological levels where molecular processes sustain cellular order through fidelity (DNA replication), service (protein synthesis), and cooperative interaction. Each level exists for the welfare of the others and is sustained by higher order integration.

A fractal architecture has a constitutive consequence: Local understanding confers global orientation. When the governing pattern is grasped at one level, it becomes intelligible at others. This is why personal moral decisions possess cosmic significance, why love and service scale upward without distortion, and why a life lived faithfully within finite conditions can disclose universal reality. Meaning learned in one context illuminates others because the same relational logic recurs throughout the whole.

Within this framework, the universe is not merely organized for persons; it is organized *like* persons—relationally, developmentally, and meaningfully—at every level. This displaces metaphysical systems that tend toward upward collapse, including forms of Gnosticism, Neoplatonism, and mystical absorption, in which transcendence overwhelms personal agency.

The cosmos illuminated by The Urantia Book is neither totalizing nor impersonal. It preserves distinction, freedom, and growth by structuring reality itself as a network of personal relationships.

Within such an order, personality remains the keystone reality. Energy, mind, and spirit function as environmental supports for personal decision and development. This is why The Urantia Book can describe a universe of immense scale without dissolving the significance of individual life. Vastness does not negate intimacy when structure is relational.

Because the same pattern governs at every level, coherence does not require centralized control, impersonal law, or static hierarchy. A personal universe cannot be managed mechanically. Coordination must preserve freedom while sustaining growth across radically different scales. The fractal form accomplishes this by repeating the same functional logic—authority as service, coordination without coercion—wherever order is required. Scale changes; function does not.

This clarifies how the three strands of our fundamental ontology—personalism, ascension, and administration—operate together. Personalism identifies what is real; ascension describes developmental movement; administration provides the ordered environment in which that movement can proceed without collapse. The fractal character of administration explains how this environment remains coherent from the smallest relational unit to the largest cosmic domain.

Within The Urantia Book's cosmology, the cumulative result of this coordinated structure is the progressive integration of values into reality itself. The authors refer to this process as *the actualization of the Supreme Being*—an emerging level of experiential Deity that reflects the fruits of finite experience. This theme marks one of The Urantia Book's most distinctive theological explications—the reality of experiential Deity and its relationship to existential Deity. A full treatment of the topic lies well beyond the present discussion. Here it is mentioned as an orienting horizon: the assurance that values generated through personal decision and lived relationships are conserved, integrated, and carried forward.

CHAPTER 8:
CALIBRATION IN A PERSONAL UNIVERSE

Calibration, as used here, names the ongoing alignment of personal freedom with a stable value-referent that renders growth meaningful over time—orientation to transcendent ideals.

A personal universe cannot be governed as an impersonal system. Law and mechanism may regulate processes, but persons require calibration: a reference that keeps freedom meaningful and development coherent.

Without calibration, meaning fragments, direction dissipates, and relationship destabilizes. Calibration is not the transmission of information or the imposition of structure. It presupposes an ideal that functions as a horizon rather than a terminal goal—an ideal which cannot be fully attained but which can be increasingly approximated. The point is not perfection achieved, but direction preserved. Because the calibrating ideal is inexhaustible, it can unify striving across persons without collapsing difference into uniformity, and it can sustain endurance without requiring final arrival.

One does not possess the calibration point; one orients to it repeatedly as experience unfolds. It becomes a lodestar for both personal and collective life.

At the level of individual experience, the Divine Indweller serves this calibrating function by continuously referencing finite decisions to enduring standards of truth, goodness, and beauty without displacing personal freedom. The Indweller does not override choice or dictate outcomes; it holds decision in relation to values, preserving proportion amid complexity.

At the universe level, Jesus functions as a calibration presence of a different scale. He is not a mechanism of governance, but the lived embodiment of what it means to exist rightly as a person within reality. In this role, Jesus provides a concrete personal reference by which freedom, authority, service, and growth can be held together without abstraction.

Understood this way, the Spirit Indweller and Jesus are not competing authorities but scale-differentiated calibration presences. Each stabilizes meaning and development by holding finite life in relation to an inexhaustible ideal appropriate to its scale.

Universe administration remains indispensable but distinct. Administration does not define values it protects the conditions under which values can be discovered through relationship, moral choice, and personal response to reality. Governance at its highest therefore takes the form of preserving alignment rather than enforcing control. It keeps reality stable enough to trust, flexible enough for growth, and personal enough to sustain meaning.

This logic culminates in the Universal Father as the final calibration point of all reality. Sovereignty here names the ultimate reference of meanings and values, not coercion. To say that the Father rules a universe of universes by the power of his love is not devotional excess but ontological precision. Love functions as the supreme alignment through which reality remains trustworthy, growth endurable, and personality preservable.

Taken together, these calibration presences disclose a coherent personal architecture: individual freedom held in relation to values by the Divine Indweller; universe life oriented by the lived example of Jesus; the conditions of growth safeguarded by administration; and the whole calibrated by the Father as inexhaustible source and final reference of meaning. Direction is preserved without compulsion; difference is sustained without fragmentation; growth remains possible without final closure.

Textual Calibration

For some readers, The Urantia Book itself functions as a calibrating instrument at the level of conceptual intake—*a hermeneutic of orientation*—especially when moving through philosophical, theological works and religious studies. It does not eliminate the need for critical judgment or substitute for scholarly method; it supplies a stable value-referent by which different paradigms can be weighed without being absolutized.

In this role, the book operates less as a catalog of positions to adopt than as an orienting hermeneutic: It keeps freedom of inquiry meaningful by repeatedly returning the mind to proportion—personhood over mechanism, relationship over reduction, growth over closure, and ultimacy as personal rather than impersonal.

Used this way, The Urantia Book does not compete with other sources as a rival "authority." It functions as a horizon-reference that helps the reader maintain internal coherence while engaging multiple schools, vocabularies, and metaphysical temperaments. It can clarify what is being gained in a given perspective, what is being lost, and where a concept quietly displaces personality, values, or destiny. The result is not insulation from the academic literature but greater elasticity within it: One can learn widely without drifting, and critique firmly without collapsing into cynicism.

CHAPTER 9:
JESUS OF NAZARETH AS
EMBODIED DEMONSTRATION

An Ontological Architecture Made Visible

Jesus is not presented here primarily as an ethical teacher, a religious exemplar, or a bearer of theological information. He is the embodied demonstration of how a personalist, ascendant, administered universe functions when fully inhabited.

What has been described architecturally in the preceding chapters becomes visible in his life. Personalism is lived without reservation. Ascendant growth unfolds within the limits of finitude. Relationship, value, and purpose are enacted rather than asserted.

The movement from the highest reality to the ordinary conditions of human life is not incidental. It is the same fractal-like relational logic operating across scale. What can seem abstract when stated cosmically becomes intelligible when lived personally. Meaning is not proclaimed from above but embodied from within. Divinity adapts to creature conditions without diminishing its nature.

Jesus' life demonstrates that the universe's architecture is not alien or antagonistic to human existence. It is compatible with ordinary life at its most concrete level: work, family, fatigue, frustration, loyalty, suffering, and joy. The structure of reality disclosed in The Urantia Book is shown to be livable at the point where human life actually unfolds.

The Strands Made Practicable

In Jesus, the three strands of our personalist ontology become simultaneously visible and coherent within human conditions.

Personalism is disclosed as lived relational reality rather than abstract principle. Persons are treated as ends, not means. Relationship becomes the medium of meaning.

Ascension appears not as escape from the world but as growth within it. Moral decision, service, patience, and faithfulness become the means by which enduring values are generated.

Universe administration is shown to exist in service of this lived value coherence. Authority functions to sustain growth rather than impose control.

Jesus is therefore not an additional element placed alongside the ontology. He is the point at which the ontology becomes legible as life. Remove him, and the structure may remain conceptually intact, but it loses its tested intelligibility. With him, the architecture proves itself inhabitable.

Value Coherence at Every Scale

Because Jesus lives the architecture rather than merely explaining it, he functions as the value-ontological center within which personal experience and cosmic order remain proportioned. What counts as power, authority, success, faithfulness, and greatness is clarified by lived example rather than rule.

Whatever form universe administration takes, it must remain consonant with the value reality disclosed in Jesus. Administration does not define value; it extends and protects value coherence across scale. The authority exercised in the universe becomes intelligible only insofar as it preserves the same relational logic made visible in his life.

Jesus therefore serves as the concrete reference by which meanings, values, and purpose remain aligned. Personal life finds orientation without abstraction. Cosmic order remains intelligible without coercion. What appears immense and remote is revealed to be continuous with the moral texture of ordinary life.

Personal Life Within Cosmic Order

Jesus does not stand outside the ontological structure, nor does he merely illustrate it. In his universe role, he presides within it. His life and sovereignty disclose how personal reality, divine presence, cosmic coordination, and ascendant growth belong together as a single coherent whole.

In him, the personal and the cosmic are not competing frames but mutually illuminating ones. Personal fidelity participates in cosmic meaning. Ordinary decisions contribute to enduring value. The universe is shown to be governed not by impersonal force or arbitrary decree, but by relational coherence grounded in personality.

This is the final confirmation of The Urantia Book's central claim: Reality is structured so that personal life matters—here, now, and at every scale—and the deepest truths of the cosmos can be lived without leaving the conditions of ordinary human existence.

Chapter 10:
World Transforming Implications

When personality is treated as ontologically primary and relationship as cosmologically decisive, familiar domains of life are re-read. The change is not primarily moral exhortation but interpretive reorientation: What is central, what is instrumental, and what is ultimately meaningful begin to shift.

Politics:
From Power Management to Relational Stewardship

In a mechanistic worldview, politics is the management of systems: balancing interests, allocating resources, enforcing order. Persons function as units within aggregates, and stability is achieved by regulation.

Within a relational personalist ontology, politics is reinterpreted as stewardship of the relational conditions under which persons and communities can mature. Authority is justified not by dominance or efficiency, but by its capacity to:

» Preserve personal dignity
» Enable participation
» Coordinate freedom without coercion

Institutions and law are not eliminated; their purpose is re-specified. Political success is measured not only by control or output, but by whether relationships—between citizens, cultures, and generations—become more coherent, humane, and future-bearing. Power is legitimate insofar as it serves the maturation of persons rather than the maintenance of systems for their own sake.

Technology:
From Optimization to Human-Scale Meaning

Technological culture commonly equates progress with speed, scale, and efficiency. Problems are framed as technical deficits; solutions are engineered accordingly.

A personalist ontology treats technology as instrumental rather than determinative. The primary question becomes not what can be built, but what forms of relationship a technology shapes, displaces, or makes harder to sustain.

Technology is evaluated by whether it:

» Enhances personal agency
» Deepens genuine connection
» Preserves interior life
» Supports long-horizon human development

When personality is primary, no technology is neutral. Applied science either serves the architecture of personalism or erodes it. This stance resists both technophobia and technophilia, insisting instead on human-scale discernment grounded in the primacy of lived relationships.

Education:
From Information Transfer to Personal Formation

In mechanistic models, education is efficient transmission of knowledge and skills. Success is measured by metrics, outputs, and competitiveness.

Within a personalist framework, education is formative. Its task is the cultivation of judgment, character, relational competence, and the ability to integrate experience into meaning. Knowledge remains essential, but as material for growth rather than as an end in itself. Learning is reinterpreted as:

» Dialogical rather than transactional
» Grounded in mentorship and exemplarity
» Oriented toward wisdom rather than accumulation

Education succeeds when persons emerge more capable of responsibility, discernment, and relationship—not merely more credentialed.

Economics:
From Accumulation to Contribution

Conventional economic systems often assume that value is created through production and measured through accumulation. Persons become consumers or labor units; growth becomes quantitative expansion.

A relational reading shifts attention to contribution. Value is generated not only by output, but by whether economic activity:

» Supports meaningful work
» Sustains communities
» Respects long-term human and ecological relationships

Prosperity is redefined as a society's capacity to enable persons to contribute meaningfully rather than merely to consume efficiently. Markets remain tools, but they are judged by relational outcomes rather than abstract indicators alone.

Spiritual Life:
From Privatization to Indwelling-Mediated Participation

In many modern settings, spirituality is privatized—reduced to interior belief or emotional reassurance and detached from any coherent account of reality. Interior life becomes subjective rather than participatory.

Within The Urantia Book model, spiritual life is indwelling-mediated participation in a personal universe. A divine presence addresses personality from within, orienting experience toward values without coercing freedom. Growth occurs through engagement: learning how to live in alignment with the evolving relational fabric of existence.

Spiritual maturity is measured less by belief intensity than by relational depth and by the integration of experience into enduring personal meaning, expressed in the visible fruits of a life lived in response to inner guidance.

History:
From Inevitability to Responsibility

This framework also re-reads history. History is no longer a neutral sequence or an inevitable march toward a predetermined outcome. What persons choose and enact matters—privately and cosmically—because reality is partly co-created through personal decision.

Growth is meaningful because experience is conserved. Hope is rational because reality is structured to receive and integrate values. History becomes participatory rather than accidental, and responsibility replaces inevitability.

Conclusion:
Orientation as Framework

The implications traced in the preceding pages—social, moral, spiritual, and civilizational—follow from a single claim: Reality is personal at its core and therefore intelligible, trustworthy, and oriented toward growth.

A personalist ontology does not promise ease, certainty, or uniformity of outcome. What it offers instead is something rarer and more durable: a universe in which persons are real, values are conserved, and experience is not wasted. The transformations envisioned here do not arise from technique or reform alone, but from a reorientation of how reality itself is understood and inhabited.

What we have reached here is not a conclusion, but orientation to reality's coherent architecture and an invitation to explore it at greater depth.

We began in Chapter 1 with a diagnosis that is difficult to deny: The contemporary Western mind is not merely uninformed but unmoored—awash in signals, skilled at analysis, fluent in options, yet starved for a frame of reference that can be *internalized* and lived within. Information multiplies while meaning thins; process is celebrated while purpose is disavowed; spiritual seeking intensifies while continuity evaporates. The result is not laziness or bad will, but fragmentation: life reduced to episodes, reactions, and improvisations; the self forced to carry the full weight of orientation alone.

Against that civilizational backdrop, The Urantia Book matters in a very specific way. It offers neither another technique for self-management, nor another ideology to compete in the marketplace of interpretations. It illuminates the world in which we live with a personalist cosmology spacious enough to integrate knowledge and meaning, change and direction, spiritual experience and continuity. It restores a durable horizon: reality as fundamentally personal and relational; growth as real and conserved; destiny as a long arc in which experience is gathered, integrated, and carried forward rather than endlessly restarted.

This is why its gift is timely. A fragmented culture does not need louder arguments; it needs a deeper architecture—an order of reality that can be inhabited, not merely admired. If the modern crisis is dislocation, then the remedy is not more motion but true orientation: a framework that stabilizes the self without shrinking it, that honors freedom without abandoning teleology, that allows the soul to develop not as perpetual reinvention but as sustained ascent.

So the end of this volume is a threshold. Not because every question has been answered, but because the reader has been given a place to stand. The purpose here has been preparatory: to name the kind of universe The Urantia Book presupposes, the kind of person it addresses, and the kind of growth it treats as real. What follows from here is not mastery but a choice of entry—exploring meanings and discovering values by living within the horizon it discloses.

If you choose to cross the threshold, step through in the right spirit: not as an extractor of information or a hunter of proofs, but as a person willing to test whether a larger order of reality may be waiting to be inhabited. Read slowly enough for the architecture to appear; read honestly enough for your own life to become part of the evidence.

Appendix I:
Schools of Personalism Compared

Below is a concise, structured inventory of major contemporary schools of personalism, each paired with a representative thinker who crystallizes its distinctive orientation. The aim is definitional clarity and the provision points of entry for those who may wish to explore further.

Boston Personalism (Metaphysical Personalism)

- » Core claim: Personality is the ultimate metaphysical reality; the universe is intelligible only as personal.
- » Key thinker: Borden Parker Bowne

French Personalism (Communitarian / Ethical)

- » Core claim: The person is realized in community, commitment, and responsibility.
- » Key thinker: Emmanuel Mounier

Polish Personalism (Act-Centered)

- » Core claim: The person is disclosed through action, self-determination, and moral choice.
- » Key thinker: Karol Wojtyła (Pope John Paul II)

German Value Personalism

- » Core claim: Persons are bearers and recognizers of value prior to rational calculation.
- » Key thinker: Max Scheler

Phenomenological Personalism

- » Core claim: Personhood is known through empathy, lived experience, and interiority.
- » Key thinker: Edith Stein

Dialogical Personalism

- » Core claim: Personhood arises in the I–Thou relation, not in isolated subjectivity.
- » Key thinker: Martin Buber

British Idealist Personalism

- » Core claim: Reality is ultimately personal, not merely logical or material.
- » Key thinker: Andrew Seth Pringle-Pattison

Existential Personalism

- » Core claim: The person is a mystery to be lived, not a problem to be solved.
- » Key thinker: Gabriel Marcel

Orthodox Trinitarian Personalism

- » Core claim: Being itself is communion; personhood precedes essence.
- » Key thinker: John Zizioulas

Process-Relational Personalism

- » Core claim: Persons (including God) are fundamentally relational and, in some respect, becoming.
- » Key thinker: Charles Hartshorne

Relational-Ontological Personalism

- » The Urantia Book

Relational-Ontological Personalism is an apt descriptor for The Urantia Book because it treats personhood and relationship as metaphysically primitive rather than late-emerging features of an otherwise impersonal evolutionary process. Personality is not explained as a byproduct of matter, mechanism, or social construction. It is presented as an ultimate category of reality, and reality is rendered intelligible in personal terms.

At the same time, this personalism is not individualism. Persons are depicted as inherently relational—constituted and fulfilled through living circuits of communion, moral choice, and value-responsive interaction across multiple orders of association. In this sense, *relational* names the claim that relationship is not merely ethical counsel or spiritual sentiment but a structural feature of reality. *Ontological* names the stronger claim that this personal-relational order belongs to the architecture of being.

The term therefore captures The Urantia Book's distinctive synthesis: a universe whose deepest intelligibility is personal, and whose personal reality is realized, conserved, and expanded through relationship.

APPENDIX II:
PERSONALISM IN CHRISTIANITY

Orthodox-Trinitarian, Catholic, and Urantia Book Registers Compared

This appendix situates The Urantia Book's Relational-Ontological Personalism (ROP) alongside two major Christian personalist registers: Orthodox-Trinitarian Personalism (OTP) and Catholic Personalism (CP). The purpose is clarification: showing where these primary Christian paradigms share a personalist grammar and where they diverge in their treatment of history, value, and destiny.

Catholic personalism and *Orthodox-Trinitarian Personalism* are used descriptively rather than confessionally. They name philosophically developed anthropological traditions that render personalist commitments especially explicit in the domains of dignity, conscience, freedom, and communal life.

Comparative Matrix of Key Structural Elements

Ultimate ground:

- » OTP: Reality is grounded in the eternally complete communion of Father, Son, and Spirit; personal relation constitutes the deepest grammar of being.

- » CP: Reality is grounded in the same eternally complete Triune communion; created persons are ordered toward participation in that divine life.

- » ROP: Reality is grounded in existential Deity (the Universal Father) and coordinated through an administered cosmos that enables an experiential axis of Deity to actualize through history.

Status of relation:

- » OTP: Communion is ontologically prior to history; creatures are invited into an already fulfilled divine relational life.

- » CP: Communion is primordial in God and freely entered by the person through grace; relation is realized historically as a formed life of love.

> » ROP: Communion is eternally purposed but temporally realized; relational fullness emerges through experience and is coordinated across scales.

Personhood:

> » OTP: Personhood is irreducible; distinctness is preserved and perfected through communion rather than dissolved by it.
> » CP: The person is irreducible—never a mere means—an interior subject capable of truth, responsibility, and love; distinctness is fulfilled within communion.
> » ROP: Personality is ontologically constant and non-evolutionary, yet developmentally expressive; destiny is co-created through long integration of experience without loss of identity.

Unity:

> » OTP: Unity is communion without absorption; wholeness intensifies participation while preserving distinctness.
> » CP: Unity is communion in truth and love, not fusion; wholeness without absorption, expressed as solidarity, fidelity, and mutual presence.
> » ROP: Unity is progressively achieved as values discovered in experience are integrated; unity is cumulative synthesis, not merely an eternal given.

Change and Becoming:

> » OTP: God does not become what God is; history does not add ontological content to Deity but is the arena of redemption and participation.
> » CP: God does not become; what becomes is the person. History is where freedom is educated, wounds are healed, and the person is conformed to divine life.
> » ROP: Existential Deity remains complete, yet experiential Deity genuinely grows through creature experience without destabilizing the existential ground.

Values and Freedom:

> » OTP: Values are grounded in eternal divine life and disclosed through grace; freedom is responsive participation—creaturely consent within a stable horizon of meaning.

» CP: Freedom is self-determination ordered to truth and the good; values are recognized and embodied, not invented; selfhood is intensified through self-gift.

» ROP: Values are discovered in indwelt life, freely chosen, conserved in the soul, and integrated into an expanding experiential reality; freedom is creatively consequential.

Mediation:

» OTP: Participation is mediated through Spirit and through ecclesial, sacramental, and communal forms of life that habituate persons into communion over time.

» CP: Communion is mediated through Christ, the Spirit's interior work, and the Church's sacramental and communal life—Word, worship, discipline, works of mercy—forming stable dispositions of love.

» ROP: Indwelling (Thought Adjuster) provides interior, non-coercive guidance, coordinated with an administered universe structure that preserves growth conditions.

Teleology and Eschatology:

» OTP: The telos is consummated communion: history gathered and fulfilled, not extended as an open-ended developmental synthesis.

» CP: The telos is personal fulfillment in communion: consummation rather than endless revision, where love is completed and the history of freedom is gathered.

» ROP: Teleology is ascendant: Persons traverse a developmental career whose fulfillment is continuing growth without terminal stasis, identity enlarged without absorption.

Collapse Risk Avoided By:

» OTP: Eternal divine completeness secures meaning and prevents both coercive transcendence and the evaporation of transcendence into mere immanent closure.

» CP: God's primacy and the inviolability of the person prevent authoritarian transcendence (the person crushed) and flattened immanent closure (the person dissolved into functions or feelings).

» ROP: Architectural mediation—indwelling plus universe administration—buffers transcendence from overwhelming finitude and prevents transcendence from dissolving into immanent closure.

Communion as the Shared Personalist Core

Across OTP, CP, and ROP, a common personalist grammar appears:

- » Persons are real and primary.
- » Relation is constitutive, not secondary.
- » Unity is communion that deepens shared life without erasing distinction.
- » Values are real, recognizable, and livable.

What differs is the relation of communion to history:

- » OTP: Meaning is secured "vertically" in eternal divine completeness.
- » CP: The vertical anchor is translated into moral formation and communal life.
- » ROP: Communion is carried "horizontally" through time as developmental, value-conservative participation.

The Urantia Book Distinction

OTP and CP secure meaning by anchoring it above historical flux: What is most real is not finally at the mercy of time. ROP shares this vertical axis, but insists that communion must also be carried forward through history—through growth, choice, and the conservation of experiential value. Read together, these registers form a widened aperture in which communion is simultaneously:

- » Eternally grounded (OTP)
- » Morally embodied (CP)
- » Historically extended (ROP)

In that widened frame, what is chosen in faith can endure, mature, and become luminous across the long arc of reality.

APPENDIX III:
THE ROOTS OF THE PERSONALIST HERITAGE

Christian personalisms are the cumulative yield of long reflection on the nature of the Trinity and the implications of Jesus' personalist teaching. Their foundational claim is that reality is ultimately disclosed in personal relationships, not impersonal mechanisms.

The Urantia Book's *Relational-Ontological Personalism* is best read against this background: It shares the Christian personalist grammar while extending it into a cosmological, developmental register.

What follows is a disciplined, lineage-based map of the major sources most often cited—or functionally operative—in contemporary personalist discourse. It is organized for orientation rather than exhaustive coverage.

I. Orthodox-Trinitarian Personalism

Early lineages and sources that establish "being as communion"

A. Patristic and Classical Foundations

These figures do not use "personalism" as a category, but they establish the ontological grammar which later OTP explicitly develops.

- » Gregory of Nazianzus: Clarified irreducible hypostasis as relational within the Trinity
- » Basil of Caesarea: Sharpened the distinction between ousia (essence) and hypostasis (person)
- » Gregory of Nyssa: Developed Trinitarian relational ontological reasoning without subordinationism
- » Augustine of Hippo: Interior Trinitarian analogies (memory–intellect–will); personal interiority before God.

Contribution: Personhood is constituted in relation; unity is communion without absorption; Trinity as calibration.

B. Nineteenth–Early Twentieth-Century Precursors

Figures who resist Enlightenment individualism and impersonal metaphysics by re-centering conscience, lived faith, and personal encounter

- » John Henry Newman: Conscience and personal assent; faith and knowledge as irreducibly personal acts
- » Friedrich Schleiermacher: Religious experience as personal consciousness (proto-personalist in method, not fully Trinitarian in ontology)

Contribution: Shifts emphasis from system to lived personal responsiveness.

C. Twentieth-Century Explicit Orthodox-Trinitarian Personalists

This is the core canon in contemporary OTP reception:

- » Vladimir Lossky: Personal distinctness; apophatic restraint; person not reducible to essence; being as communion; personhood as relationally constituted existence
- » Christos Yannaras: Relational freedom and critique of individualism

Contribution: Makes communion the primary category for being; secures transcendence without coercion and unity without fusion.

D. Protestant Contributions

Selective, but structurally influential in the modern personal-address register: Here truth is not only *said,* but spoken to *someone*—and it therefore calls for response, not mere assent.

- » Karl Barth: Revelation as personal self-disclosure; relation grounded in the Triune life
- » Dietrich Bonhoeffer: Responsibility before God and others; personhood realized in relation and obedience.
- » Emil Brunner: Encounter as core: Revelation is fundamentally personal meeting; faith is response to address, not assent to a system.
- » Thomas F. Torrance: Revelation is understood as an event of encounter between persons.

Contribution: Strengthens the grammar of personal address and moral responsibility within history.

II. Catholic Personalism

Lineages and sources that translate Trinitarian communion into moral anthropology

A. Classical and Medieval Resources Repeatedly Retrieved

These figures supply conceptual resources later Catholic personalists adapt rather than abandon:

- » Boethius: Baseline definition of "person" as a primary point of departure

- » Augustine of Hippo: Interiority, will, irreducible subject before God
- » Thomas Aquinas: Nature/person distinctions; participation metaphysics usable against depersonalization
- » Bonaventure: Affective-relational knowing; personhood oriented toward love and communion

Contribution: Provides a durable metaphysical and theological grammar—person, participation, interiority, relationality

B. Nineteenth and Early Twentieth-Century Precursors

Figures who re-center conscience, action, and lived commitment against reductionism:

- » John Henry Newman: Conscience and assent as personal acts
- » Antonio Rosmini: Dignity and rights grounded in personalist anthropology
- » Maurice Blondel: Philosophy of action; transcendence becomes existentially unavoidable in the acting subject

Contribution: Makes the person-as-agent methodologically primary; resists the reduction of meaning to system

C. Twentieth-Century Explicit Catholic Personalists

Three major streams commonly cited or functionally operative:

1) French social and communitarian personalism

- » Emmanuel Mounier: Person-in-community; alternative to individualism and collectivism
- » Jacques Maritain: Person versus individual; Christian humanism; cultural and political implications
- » Maurice Nédoncelle: Reciprocity and interpersonal consciousness as central
- » Gabriel Marcel: Fidelity, availability, interpersonal mystery
- » Paul Ricœur: Personalist concerns historically adjacent, even when not branded as such

2) Realist Phenomenology of Value and Interiority

- » Max Scheler: Value theory; person as center of acts
- » Dietrich von Hildebrand: Value-response, love, moral consciousness

» Edith Stein: Empathy, community, personhood integrated with Catholic commitments

3) Polish/Lublin Act-Centered Personalism

» Karol Wojtyła (John Paul II): Acting person: self-determination and self-gift
» Mieczysław A. Krąpiec: Realist metaphysical personalism
» Tadeusz Styczeń: Conscience and normativity
» Andrzej Szostek: Moral anthropology in the Wojtyłan line

Contribution (the Catholic synthesis): Personalism becomes explicit as an anthropological-ethical register: the person as irreducible subject, value-responsive, freedom-capable, inherently relational, and ordered to communion—developed as social vision, value-phenomenology, and act-centered moral anthropology.

D. Dialogical and Relational Allies Often Appropriated

Figures who sharpen the interpersonal lexicon used across personalist discourse

» Martin Buber: I–Thou as fundamental interpersonal grammar
» Ferdinand Ebner: Language and address as constitutive of personhood and God-relation
» Franz Rosenzweig: Encounter and revelation in dialogical form
» Emmanuel Levinas: Primacy of the Other; radical responsibility (often engaged critically)

Contribution: A refined vocabulary of address is supplied: presence, encounter, reciprocity, and responsibility.

Integrating Note: Where ROP Sits Relative to These Roots

ROP shares the Christian personalist core claims that (1) persons are primary, (2) relation is ontologically serious, and (3) communion does not erase distinctness. Its distinctive move is to render this grammar cosmological and developmental: personal destiny unfolds through time; value is not only recognized and embodied but conserved and integrated across extended horizons; and transcendence is mediated through indwelling and universe administration so that growth remains possible without coercion or flattening.

Values: A Shared Commitment

OTP, CP, and ROP converge on a decisive claim: Values are not private projections or social conveniences, but realities to be recognized and embodied—objective in status, personal in appropriation. Their objectivity does not make them impersonal; it means they are answerable, ordered, and carry real moral weight.

Yet values are disclosed most deeply through personal modes of access—conscience, encounter, worship, fidelity, and responsible action—because persons are the beings for whom values can appear as claim and calling. OTP grounds values in the luminous character of ultimate communion; CP tracks values through moral anthropology, conscience, and the dignity of the acting person. ROP extends these commitments into a cosmological-developmental horizon in which values are not only recognized and enacted, but conserved and integrated as lasting personal attainment.

Appendix IV:
Glossary

Working Definitions Used in This Volume

Each entry below does three things: (1) stabilizes usage in this present work, (2) distinguishes the term from nearby meanings, and (3) ties it to The Urantia Book's personalist architecture.

Ascension

» In common usage: "Going up" (afterlife, exaltation, spiritual elevation) without a precise ontology

» In this volume: The developmental trajectory of enduring personality; progressive growth through choice, relationship, and value-integration across extended horizons

» Not: Escape from finitude; absorption into an impersonal absolute; an externally imposed reward

» Architectural role: Presupposes (a) enduring personality (a real subject who persists), (b) value-generative experience (choices matter), and (c) coordinated cosmic order (growth can scale beyond mortal life)

Destiny

» In common usage: Fate, foreordination, inevitable outcome

» In this volume: Co-created purpose; the realization of personality through freely chosen experience in cooperation with divine leading and a value-conserving order

» Not: A fixed script; mere "life planning"; prediction

» Architectural role: What personality becomes as meanings are translated into lived values and gathered into a coherent personal career

Ecological

» In common usage: Environmental concern, or loose "systems talk"

» In this volume: Relational architecture of interdependence; reality coheres through living, coordinated relations in which persons develop and values become transmissible and cumulative

» Not: Impersonal mechanism; a metaphor for "connectedness" with no ontological weight

» Architectural role: The shape of a personal universe; Growth through participation, coordination, and mutual responsiveness rather than domination or extraction

Eschatological

» In common usage: End-times, final judgment, terminal closure
» In this volume: The teleological horizon of fulfillment; developmental consummation rather than catastrophic termination; personal destiny as continuing realization rather than "the end of history"
» Not: Apocalyptic timetable; purely symbolic hope; juridical finality as the controlling frame
» Architectural role: Reframes "last things" as mature outcomes of long growth: evaluation intrinsic to development; fulfillment as deepening participation

Ex Nihilo

» In common usage: From nothing, used as a master-explanation for all novelty
» In this volume: Affirmed as a claim about ultimate source, but insufficient for describing how meanings and values arise within experience
» Not: A description of character growth, moral development, or the generation of lived meaning
» Architectural role: Protects divine ultimacy as source while leaving room for experiential realization; values arise through cooperation; personality, indwelling, and an ordered environment conserve outcomes

Existentialism

» In common usage: Philosophies emphasizing lived existence, anxiety, freedom, responsibility
» In this volume: A diagnosis of late-modern dislocation; freedom without ontological support; meaning carried by the self alone when transcendence is culturally unavailable
» Not: A single doctrine you must accept or reject; a caricature of despair
» Architectural role: Retains existential seriousness (choice, responsibility) while supplying the missing ground; a personal universe where meaning is discovered and conserved, not fabricated and lost

Existential Deity

- » In common usage: Not a standard classical term; often confused with "the God of philosophers"
- » In this volume: Ultimate reality as complete in being; self-existent, not dependent on time, process, or creature experience for actuality
- » Not: An impersonal absolute; a remote perfection indifferent to persons
- » Architectural role: Secures stability: reality as trustworthy; meaning as not hostage to flux; personality as bestowed rather than manufactured or evolved

Experiential Deity

- » In common usage: Easily confused with process theology or divine change as deficiency
- » In this volume: The mode in which finite experience yields conserved value—history as contributing genuinely new realized content without destabilizing existential divine completeness
- » Not: God becoming "more God" by needing the world; ultimacy reduced to process
- » Architectural role: Answering the "so what" of moral and spiritual life; choices and relationships are not merely private; accrual and endurance of values

Fractal-Like Architecture

- » In common usage: A mathematical metaphor (self-similarity across scales)
- » In this volume: An interpretive term for the book's recursive relational pattern: coordination without coercion; authority as service; similar logic expressed across levels without making levels identical
- » Not: A claim that everything looks the same; a mechanistic "pattern of control"
- » Architectural role: Explains how local moral life can illuminate cosmic order; scale changes; relational logic remains legible

Hermeneutic

- » In common usage: A theory of interpretation (especially of texts)

- » In this volume: The interpretive posture appropriate to an inhabitable framework: personalist, participatory, developmental—tested by coherence, integration, and fruitfulness in lived life
- » Not: Authoritarian literalism; relativistic projection
- » Architectural role: Interpretation and personal growth as inseparable from a conceptual framework

Hypostasis

- » In common usage: Individual instance; concrete reality; person; the "who" that remains the same even as their feelings, roles, and circumstances change.
- » In this volume: Irreducible personal center of agency and relationship—identity that endures through experience while remaining open to communion and development
- » Not: Mere role, mask, or psychological profile; an isolated atom sealed off from others; a detachable "part" of a larger whole
- » Architectural role: Grounds personal distinctiveness within relational unity: it preserves the "who" of existence so that growth, responsibility, and reciprocal address occur without absorption or fragmentation

Imago Dei

- » In common usage: "Humans resemble God" (often reduced to one faculty: reason, dominion, morality)
- » In this volume: The ontological dignity of the person: capacity for relationship with God and others, value-recognition, moral agency, and growth—without collapsing the Creator–creature distinction
- » Not: Physical resemblance; divinity by nature; moral perfection already achieved
- » Architectural role: Grounds personal worth prior to performance, utility, or social role; supports the claim that personality is real and teleologically oriented

Immanent Closure

- » In common usage: Secular sufficiency or closed-system naturalism; reality treated as self-contained, with "beyond" excluded from consideration

» In this volume: Loss of vertical ultimacy; transcendence no longer relevant; indwelling presence no longer salient; meanings and values remain in the horizontal dimension

» Not: Theological immanence (divine nearness); pantheism or panentheism; mature interiority that remains open to transcendence

» Architectural role: Names the primary occlusion; guidance and communion are experienced as unavailable; purpose thins into process without a vertical horizon

Indwelling

» In common usage: Vague interior spirituality; sometimes mystical fusion

» In this volume: The Thought Adjuster as defined in The Urantia Book: an interior divine presence that guides non-coercively through mind, without inhabiting or replacing personality

» Not: Personality "possessed" by God; conscience as mere psychology; coercive control

» Architectural role: Supplies the interior vertical axis: meanings clarify, values take hold, the soul forms, and destiny becomes co-created

Nihilism

» In common usage: "Nothing matters," often treated as a mood or moral failure

» In this volume: A structural outcome of inadequate ontology: if persons do not endure and personal experience conserves nothing, meaning cannot accumulate and value becomes arbitrary

» Not: A label for people; not merely depression or cynicism

» Architectural role: Clarifies what The Urantia Book framework is answering: how meaning can be real, durable, and publicly consequential.

Ontology

» In common usage: Inquiry into what is real.
In this volume: The ground of being and the architecture of reality—the underlying order that determines what can exist, how things relate, and why experience coheres rather than dissolves into fragments.

» Not: A detachable theory with no existential consequences

» Architectural role: The present work's conceptual hinge: personalism, ascension, and administration as the load-bearing features of an inhabitable reality

Ousia

» In common usage: Essence; substance; what something *is* at the level of being rather than appearance
» In this volume: The underlying ontological field that makes personal existence possible—being as the stable ground within which personality endures and relations unfold
» Not: A static "stuff" out of which things are made; an impersonal substrate that erases individuality; a materialistic substance theory
» Architectural role: Secures continuity and intelligibility across change: It names the depth-dimension of reality that allows growth, differentiation, and personal participation without dissolution into flux

Personalism

» In common usage: A broad family of theoretical perspectives about the primacy of persons
» In this volume: An defining ontological claim: Personality is irreducible and primary; relationship is constitutive; meanings and values are disclosed through lived participation rather than reduced to mechanism or mere subjectivity
» Not: Sentimentality; individualism; a merely ethical "be nice" program
» Architectural role: Establishes what is ultimately real: persons-in-relation within a personal universe

Praxis

» In common usage: "Practice," often politicized or reduced to technique
» In this volume: Lived enactment of an inhabitable framework: action that embodies interior orientation—truth lived, values chosen, relationship sustained
» Not: External compliance; mere activism; ritual detached from transformation
» Architectural role: Where revelation influences culture: It shows up in what a person becomes and contributes through service

Recursion

- » In common usage: Repetition, circularity
- » In this volume: Structured re-application of the same relational logic across levels (the engine of the fractal-like description)
- » Not: Redundancy: self-referential loops with no development
- » Architectural role: Explains how order scales without coercion: Coordination repeats; content varies by level and maturity

Relational-ontological

- » In common usage: Relationality is ontologically primary (not merely descriptive).
- » In this volume: Relation is not an add-on to already complete entities; it belongs to the architecture of being. Personality endures; relationship is the medium of its realization.
- » Not: Dissolving identity into relations; atomistic identity with relations as optional
- » Architectural role: Prevents both failures at once—isolated selfhood and absorptive unity

Relational-ontological personalism

- » In common usage: Not used
- » In this volume: The combined claim that (1) personality is ontologically primary and enduring and (2) relationship is constitutive, developmental, and value-bearing—history matters because experience is conserved and integrated
- » Not: A mere school-label; process reduction; static metaphysics
- » Architectural role: names the framework the reader is invited to inhabit, not merely analyze

Secularism

- » In common usage: Separation of church and state; or denial of God
- » In this volume: The late-modern condition where transcendence becomes publicly non-operative: Meaning is privatized, ontology thins, persons carry the weight of existence alone
- » Not: A synonym for atheism
- » Architectural role: Supplies the cultural backdrop for fragmentation: When transcendence is functionally removed, existential drift and nihilism become live pressures

Supremacy

- » In common usage: Dominance or control (often morally charged)
- » In this volume: The experiential integration of values: achieved coherence of history's meanings and values, not coercive rule; the actualization of experiential Deity
- » Not: Domination; static hierarchy
- » Architectural role: Anchors why nothing of genuine value is lost: Finite experience can be gathered into an enlarging whole.

Teleological

- » In common usage: Purpose-driven, sometimes confused with determinism
- » In this volume: Direction without predetermination: Reality is oriented toward ends, but fulfillment is achieved through free personal creative engagement, not imposed scripts.
- » Not: Fate; mechanistic design; arbitrary "self-made purpose"
- » Architectural role: Keeps growth intelligible: Freedom is gathered into purpose rather than severed from it.

Thought Adjuster

- » In common usage: Not used
- » In this volume: Urantia Book-specific terminology for the divine indweller: a prepersonal fragment of the Universal Father indwelling mortal mind—guiding, spiritualizing, and conserving values—without inhabiting personality or replacing will
- » Not: Conscience alone; an "inner voice" as psychology; mystical fusion
- » Architectural role: The interior mechanism of participation: the personal bridge between transcendence and lived growth

Transcendence

- » In common usage: "Beyond," often implying distance
- » In this volume: a designator for spiritual realities on the vertical axis of human experience beyond materialism and psychological determinism—levels of the real not exhaustively explainable by physics, biology, or psychology
- » Not: Remote absolutism; anti-world spirituality; denial of immanence

> » Architectural role: Restores vertical orientation; ultimacy and higher orders of value kept spiritually alive; flattening into material or psychological sufficiency prevented

Ultimacy

> » In common usage: Final meaning, absolute, terminal endpoint, no further reduction possible
> » In this volume: The comprehensive horizon within which personality, relationship, experience, and growth are unified without loss of distinction; permanence capable of receiving fulfillment
> » Not: Frozen finality; an impersonal absolute indifferent to history
> » Architectural role: Holds together what modernity often splits—stability and growth; transcendence and immanence; unity and plurality

SELECTED WORKS
CONSULTED AND RECOMMENDED

This volume employs no formal citations. What follows is a selective list of works which helped shape the orientation presented herein—titles read or consulted during manuscript creation, along with some included as especially useful entry points. The aim is not to document quotations or line-by-line dependence, but to situate this work within a wider conversation and to offer readers dependable pathways into the core literature.

Auxier, Randall E. "God, Process, and Persons: Charles Hartshorne and Personalism." In *Hartshorne and Brightman on God, Process, and Persons: The Correspondence, 1922–1945*, edited by Randall E. Auxier and Mark Y. A. Davies, 100–120. Nashville: Vanderbilt University Press, 2001.

Bowne, Borden Parker. *Personalism*. Boston and New York: Houghton, Mifflin and Company, 1908.

Buber, Martin. *I and Thou*. Translated by Walter Kaufmann. New York: Charles Scribner's Sons, 1970.

Burgos, Juan Manuel. *An Introduction to Personalism*. Washington, DC: The Catholic University of America Press, 2018.

Crosby, John F. *The Selfhood of the Human Person*. Washington, DC: The Catholic University of America Press, 1996.

Dulles, Avery, S.J. *Revelation Theology: A History*. New York: Herder and Herder, 1969.

Dulles, Avery, S.J. *Models of Revelation*. 2nd ed. Maryknoll, NY: Orbis Books, 1992.

Grosso, Andrew. Personal Being: Polanyi, Ontology, and Christian Theology. Oxford: Oxford University Press, 2019.

Lossky, Vladimir. *The Mystical Theology of the Eastern Church*. Translated by the Fellowship of St. Alban and St. Sergius. Crestwood, NY: St. Vladimir's Seminary Press, 1976.

Niebuhr, H. Richard. *The Meaning of Revelation*. New York: Macmillan, 1941.

Patterson, Andrew R. Chalcedonian Personalism: Rethinking the Human. Grand Rapids, MI: William B. Eerdmans Publishing Company, 2023.

Rahner, Karl. "Revelation." In *Sacramentum Mundi: An Encyclopedia of Theology*, edited by Karl Rahner et al., vol. 5, 349–357. New York: Herder and Herder, 1969.

Rahner, Karl. *The Trinity*. Translated by Joseph Donceel. New York: Herder and Herder, 1970.

Rolnick, Philip A. *Person, Grace, and God: A Theology of Relationality*. Grand Rapids, MI: William B. Eerdmans Publishing Company, 2011.

Shepherd, Victor A. *The Committed Self: An Introduction to Existentialism for Christians*. Toronto: BPS Books, 2015.

The Urantia Book. Indexed version. New York: Uversa Press, 2003.

Wicks, Robert L. *Introduction to Existentialism*. Oxford: Oneworld Publications, 2003.

Woznicki, Andrew N. *Karol Wojtyła's Existential Personalism*. Washington, DC: The Catholic University of America Press, 1980.

Yannaras, Christos. *The Freedom of Morality*. Translated by Elizabeth Brière. Foreword by Bishop Kallistos of Diokleia. Contemporary Greek Theologians 3. Crestwood, NY: St. Vladimir's Seminary Press, 1984.

Zizioulas, John D. *Being as Communion: Studies in Personhood and the Church*. Crestwood, NY: St. Vladimir's Seminary Press, 1985.

A Note to the Reader

I began work on an introduction to The Urantia Book in 1996. An early version appeared online in 2005 as *Toward a Jesus-Centered Study of The Urantia Book.* That first effort was broad-gauge: I set themes from systematic theology alongside parallel claims and categories in the Urantia text. Over time, my appreciation for The Urantia Book as a personalist cosmology began to take shape. Associated with this was a desire to find a common threads running through the text which could be used as an orienting introduction.

In the years since, I have continued sustained study of The Urantia Book while working more deeply within personalist topics and their theological implications as expanded by The Urantia Book. Many of the works listed in "Selected Works Consulted and Recommended" reflect that long formation.

My formal theological education was limited to a small number of audited courses at the Graduate Theological Union (Berkeley, California). The majority of my background has come through self-education and studies of theological and philosophical works which relate to themes and issues relevant to the Urantia revelation.

Several introductions to The Urantia Book have been written by readers. The majority however, only serve as book reviews which remain largely within The Urantia Book's own conceptual world. This volume has a different intent: to present The Urantia Book through philosophical and theological resources external to the text so that serious investigators—especially those conversant with modern and postmodern currents in Christian thought—can assess its world view without the baggage of assumptions about revelation.

My recent feature-length film, *When Stories Die: Christianity's Crisis and the Urantia Papers,* argues that the loss of shared story is a major driver of Christianity's contemporary decline. Many thoughtful people now live with moral and spiritual commitments but without cosmic orientation. Whatever one concludes about its origin, The Urantia Book offers an ambitious narrative architecture for re-engaging Christian meaning: It reanimates key archetypes, restores neglected horizons of interpretation, and reopens longstanding theological questions within a widened universe frame.

That is why I returned to the task of completing this introduction. I believe concerned clergy, lay leaders, and serious commentators should at least be aware of The Urantia Book as a rapidly spreading, grassroots response to Christianity's crisis of narratives. This volume is my attempt to provide that orientation.

ABOUT THE AUTHOR

David Kantor is a multimedia content creator focused on fostering informed interest in The Urantia Book. A retired software developer and a reader since 1966, his Urantia Book related work spans the production of feature-length documentary films, books, websites, conference talks, workshops, and technical papers.

With a background in music performance, photography, and professional graphics work, he began producing multiple-projector media performances in the late 1970s. As director of the multimedia division of the Family of God Foundation, he created programs for regional and national Urantia conferences.

He pioneered some of the first websites devoted to The Urantia Book and its history, providing an archive of secondary resources.

In 2018 he served as an associate editor for the Urantia Press publication, *The Untold Story of Jesus.*

As chair of The Urantia Book Fellowship's International Fellowship Committee for many years, he helped support reader conferences across Latin America—including Brazil, Chile, Colombia, Ecuador, Costa Rica, Guatemala, and Mexico—as well as Lithuania and Russia.

In 2012, he founded Urantia Book Films under the auspices of Rocky Mountain Spiritual Fellowship to develop mass-market media on Urantia Book themes. His feature length films include *Re-Imagining Jesus* (2014), shot on location in Israel and Jordan, and *When Stories Die: Christianity's Crisis and the Urantia Revelation* (2025). In 2025 Urantia Book Films began branching out into print media to supplement film work.

He is the author of *Seed, Flower, Fruit: From the Kingdom of Heaven to the Supreme Being,* and the editor of *Beside the Still Waters: 30 Psalms for Readers of The Urantia Book.* He lives in the glorious state of Colorado and is an active member of Rocky Mountain Spiritual Fellowship.